Contents

1

Preface

Conisbrough has now survived over 15 centuries of change.

This book is one man's view at a particular time. I cannot claim to have attempted the impossible task of being in touch with every source of information relating to Conisbrough, but it presents my interpretation of the subject based on material already written, plus my own observations of other places and events which, though seemingly remote, I believe are relevant. This work is not therefore merely a revision and collation of existing records, it contains additional material, some controversial, to suggest what has most likely happened in this locality.

Not being an academic, my own experience has been rather different from others who have already written on the history of Conisbrough. My career as a building and civil engineer has given me the opportunity to work in many parts of the U.K. and to travel widely, here and abroad. This has allowed me to visit and study many other sites and consider how Conisbrough was most likely affected and developed in parallel to them.

I therefore acknowledge with grateful thanks those previous historians whose chronicles have made this work possible. Also Dave Butler of the Library Service for helping me at the start of the project, in 1989, with a number of good leads, Irene MacDonald for clerical assistance work on some of my notes, Paul Raymond who I commissioned to paint "St. Paulinus preaching at Conisbrough about 630A.D." for the coverpiece, Peter Atkins who has drawn for me a pictorial map of Conisbrough and Denaby for the centrepiece, and finally to John Aird for his painstaking work of going through the text word by word and for his help in the book's layout etc.

Bernard Pearson.
D.M.S., I.Eng., A.M.I.C.E., F.I.C.W., M.I.Mgt.

3

Background

A surprising number of villages and small towns in England possess a ruined castle or monastic ruin. Here in Conisbrough we have both, and now that the castle has had new floors and roof installed in a long term renovation project, they are both in working order. The church has now been in daily use for over thirteen hundred years for worship within the same walls.

Over Conisbrough's long history little can be found to have been written about it, but by looking at other places which do have written evidence, it is possible to piece together a comparable story by using the archaeological evidence that is present today.

Of the original dwellers of Britain we know nothing. It was probably inhabited by nomadic tribes seeking new hunting fields, who came when Britain was still joined by land to the continent of Europe. These people, whoever they were, were eventually displaced by the Celts who were gradually colonising Europe from the east. They arrived in Britain about 300BC.

When Julius Caesar arrived in Britain in 55 BC he found the land divided into several kingdoms, enjoying a high standard of civilisation; an organised society, rich with cultivated land, livestock farming, and some mining of minerals. Crafts such as pottery making, wool spinning and weaving, metal and woodworking were already established. The Don and Dearne river valleys were part of the kingdom of the Brigantes which spanned from the middle of Leicester to the north of Carlisle. This area was mainly woodland and the residents probably lived in small clearings. Because of its terrain and distance from the main townships there would have been little change to its culture over hundreds of years.

It is known that the physical geography of a country has a great effect on how people live, (highlands or lowlands). In the first century AD. there was a period of relatively high sea-levels which caused much flooding throughout Europe. This was followed by a "marine regression" which dried out large areas and opened up new lands for cultivation. In this area the River Don flood plain would have dried out sufficiently for crops to be grown. Denaby is the location of an ancient crossing of the River Don near Strafford

Sands (the area now generally known as "the Pastures"). At this point a pre-historic way and a Roman road, Ricknield Street (Roman Ridge) met and crossed the river.

During the Roman Occupation, which lasted over 300 years, it was normal to allow the local ruler to continue, in association with Roman rule, providing they accepted the authority of Rome. It is known that at the time of the Roman invasion the Brigantes were ruled by a queen. She made peace with the Romans and did not take part in the rebellion led by Boadicea, therefore this part of Britain lived in peace and prosperity during the Roman Occupation. A number of its people would have joined the Roman army and would have taken administrative jobs in the Empire. All soldiers were required to be able to read and write, and would receive a pension and Roman citizenship after 20 years service. Many other Brigantes would have also been given Roman citizenship and take up Roman lifestyles. In the country, in villages such as Conisbrough, the native population would continue to live in timber built houses, but those who adopted the Roman style would live in stone dwellings in towns such as Danum (Doncaster), and Eboracum (York). This is why there have been relatively few finds of Roman artifacts in this area.

Then, in the third century AD. there was a return of the wetter climate and once again flooding of many parts of Europe. This resulted in the tribes that had been driven northwards to less productive lands by the Roman invasion, raiding the Roman-held lands for food. The Roman empire at this time had become fragmented and was finding it difficult to maintain its frontiers. This raiding and harassment continued until the first half of the fifth century when the Romans totally withdrew from Britain.

The Beginning Of Conisbrough And The English Settlement

In Britain, as the Romans moved out, the inhabitants were told by the withdrawing troops that they should take arms and redevelop the will to fight which had been lost during the Roman rule. Rome fell to the Gauls in AD470, 1164 years after its foundation. With the departure of the Roman troops the Irish attacked from the north west and the Picts came over Hadrian's Wall. A great slaughter took place. The Romano-Britons abandoned their towns and villas and fled, and with no-one to work the land, a famine resulted.

The Irish departed to their homelands taking their spoils with them while the Picts remained in the north and from time to time incursions took place. In about 449AD the leaders of the south eastern area of Britain called for help from men living in northern Germany who had not been beaten by Rome. There were three tribes, Angles, Saxons and Jutes, who responded to this call. When they had had the opportunity to look around and compare this fertile land to what their homeland had to offer, and realised how weak the Romanised Britons where, they began to settle and push the previous inhabitants westward towards Wales.

There were some Iron Age hill-forts which became temple sites in the Roman period, they lingered on with Pagan or Christian connections when the Romans began to depart. It is generally assumed that Conisbrough was one such place. With this departure there remained a nation that had lost its administrative hierarchy, and various leaders emerged who were either elected or who had conquered a region.

Geoffrey of Monmouth, a 12th century writer, whose works consist of a mixture of true historical events embroidered with fiction to present an acceptable work that would gratify the lords of the day, says of Conisbrough:-

"Conan (a Knight) began a Berg. In all the world there was not such a Berg so fair". He goes on to describe how this same Conan assisted in driving back the Pict invaders to their northern mountains and fought so bravely in the "Battle of Miesbele 494AD." About 150 years ago the Rector of Sprotborough, the Rev. Scott Surtees, presented a claim that this battle was fought on level ground between Conisbrough and Mexborough (Miesbele), but any evidence would have been lost in the 19th century with the building of the canal, railway, colliery, power station and other building works.

This area became the Kingdom of Elmet. No-one has been able to draw exact maps showing the boundaries of these Kingdoms as they were continually changing. Conisbrough was by now a principal settlement of this kingdom, and may even have been its capital judging by the later building of a minster church.

England in c.600

The invaders were withheld for over 100 years and Elmet was still controlled by Romano-Britons with their own king. The map below portrays the likely Kingdoms around 600AD.

The fortified village of Conisbrough defended one of the few places where it was then possible to ford the River Don. The area of the fort was roughly the triangle now bounded by High Street, West Street and Church Street. It had two gates, Marchgate was the one to be entered coming from the direction of what is now Newhill, with Wellgate being the rear. The boundary would have been a soil embankment with a timber balustrade along the ridge. It would have been defended by its inhabitants, a self sufficient community capable of mustering about 200 persons.

8

Sometime in the early 600's it accepted the Saxon nobleman, Edwin, exiled from the Kingdom of Deira (bordering Northumbria) as its Overlord. Edwin most probably lived here with Coenberg, the daughter of Cearl, King of the Mercians. It is not known whether the village is named after her or that she took the name of the village. They had a number of children. Within a period of about 15 years Edwin had brought under his control the north and midlands of England and he had treaties with his neighbours.

By 630AD. Conisbrough, along with Elmet, was absorbed into the province of Lindsey, part of the Northumbrian kingdoms.

The Coming Of Christianity To Conisbrough

Written sources of events for the fifth and sixth century are few and not very satisfactory, this is why they are called The Dark Ages. There is some archaeological evidence with small associated references. One text known as "The Ruin of Britain" was written in about 540 AD. by a British monk named Gildars.

The "Venerable" Bede, a Monk who spent most of his life in the Northumbrian monastery of Jarrow, completed the highly regarded "Ecclesiastical history of the English people" in 731 AD. It had taken several years to complete and is said to be based on earlier documents which regretfully have not survived.

We know from Bede that Kent was both the first Anglo-Saxon Kingdom to be established, and the first to receive Christianity.

King Ethelbert the First of Kent married a Frankish Princess named Bertha, daughter of the King of Paris. She was a Christian who was allowed to bring her chaplain with her.

Hearing of this, Pope Gregory, in 597 AD, sent from Rome a monk called Augustine. The first church in Britain since the fall of the Roman Empire was established by Augustine in Canterbury. On Pope Gregory's instructions he was consecrated "Archbishop of the English Nation" by Ethercus, Archbishop of Arles, in 600AD.

From Bede we know that what is now Yorkshire had been settled by the Angle peoples for more than a century before 600AD. They were known collectively as "the Dere" which is derived from the British word "deifn" which means "waters". This suggests that their first settlements had been along the rivers which converge on the River Humber. Their expansion towards the west was long delayed by the Britons in Elmet of which Conisbrough was a part.

In the early Autumn of 616AD there was a fierce battle fought on the southern border of Deira near the point at which the River Idle is crossed by the Roman road (Ermine Street) running from Lincoln to Doncaster. It is the first recorded trial of strength between a King of Northumberland and an Overlord of the Southern Confederation of Kingdoms.

This Overlord, Ethelfrith, who had been unable to bring all his men together for the battle, was defeated and killed.

King Edwin of Northumberland was now accepted as Overlord and within a few years his domain grew to cover much of the lands south of the River Humber in addition to his more northerly territories.

Edwin had now achieved more than any other ruler since Roman times, and by being prepared to make alliances, he gained a period of peace.

One of these alliances was made when Ethelbert, the second King of Kent gave his sister Ethelberga, to Edwin in marriage. Ethelberga would have been raised in the Christian faith by her mother, Bertha.

In 601AD Paulinus came from Rome as a young man to help Augustine, he was consecrated Bishop by Archbishop Justies on July 21st. 625.

Ethelberga was allowed to keep her faith and took Paulinus with her on her marriage. Paulinus started to preach, but it did not go well for over a year until Edwin was converted. Edwin's baptism took place at York on Easter Day, the 12th of April 627. With him, according to Bede, were Osfrid and Eadfrid, his sons by Coenburg. Other members of his household were also baptised.

We know from Bede that Paulinus and his deacon, James, preached with King Edwin's full consent in this area 628-633 AD. Conisbrough would have had some Christian converts in this period.

In 633, The British King Cadwalla rebelled against Edwin. On the 12th of October, there was a fierce battle at Hatfield. Edwin and his son Osfrid were killed and his entire army destroyed or scattered. Another son, Eadfrid, was later killed in breach of a treaty of safe keeping. Edin was 48 years old at the time of his death.

Following this battle a great slaughter took place, decimating the Northunbrian lands and the Christian followers. For the next 2 years Cadwalla tried to carry out genocide upon the entire English race.

Paulinus took Queen Ethelberga and her children by sea back to Kent where they were honourably received. Paulinus was put in charge of the church in Rochester where he died six years later. He left his deacon, James, to care for the church in the north.

During the 2 years of slaughter carried out by Cadwalla, he systematically killed all the principal heirs to the Kingdom of Northumbria. Eventually one heir, Oswald, who had been in exiled in Ireland, returned and gathered a small but very faithful Christian army. Despite being vastly outnumbered by Cadwalla's forces they engaged in battle at Denisesburn (New Rowley Water). They routed the enemy and Cadwalla was killed.

In 634 Oswald became King of Northumberland by combat. He was a Christian and had lived in Ireland for some time. This battle signified the end of Romanised-British history and subsequently determined the course of English history.

Ireland, which had had the Christian faith for over 200 years from the time of Saint Patrick had operated in isolation from the rest of the Christian church and had developed differently from the church in Rome. Women were allowed to be priests and priests were allowed to marry, but they had a devout core who neither married nor owned any property and devoted themselves entirely to their religious duties.

One such person, Aidian was sent to King Oswald after his request for a Bishop to be sent from Ireland rather than Rome.

Bede tells us that Aidian was a man of outstanding gentleness, holiness and moderation. King Oswald gave him the island of Lindisfarne to be his episcopal see in 635AD, and Aidan asked the monks of Iona (also founded by an Irish monk, St Cuthbert) for help. Their example of personal discipline, strictness in their poverty and joy in their passion for missionary work, provided the barbaric countrymen among whom they worked with a powerful and virtually irresistible force in their conversion to a Christian way of life. Over half a million people in less than 20 years were converted. Aidian always travelled on foot, and he would only have had a small number of monks to accompany him.

King Oswald was defeated and killed by King Penda of Mercia at Oswesty in 641. He was succeeded by his half brother Oswy who subsequently conquered Mercia, Sthraclyde and a large part of the Pictish kingdom. Oswy died in 670.

The Northumbrian Kingdom lasted for a further 200 years but very little is known of the later kings beyond their names.

From The Synod Of Whitby To The Viking Invasions

One of the aims of Pope Gregory was to reconcile the discipline of Rome to the Celtic Churches in English Kingdoms. The main point of contention was the method to be used to determine on what date Easter should be celebrated. At the Synod of Whitby in 664 King Oswy of Northumbria decided in favour of the Roman way. There were some Celtic traditionalists who would not accept this interpretation and so returned to their homeland. The Irish ceased sending missionaries and did not assent to the discipline of Rome at this time.

In 664 the Pope sent a new Archbishop to Canterbury, following the refusal of a few preferred nominations, a surprising candidate, a native of Asia Minor named Theodore was appointed.

During his ministry he rationalised diocesan structures and administration. A synod held at Hertford in 672 established the first Canon for the government of the church in England.

At this time one of those opposed to Theodore was Wilfred, Bishop of Ripon and then York. Wilfred was expelled from office, whereupon he made two appeals to Rome, During a turbulent life he was variously exiled and imprisoned, but he still succeeded in converting the kingdom of Sussex to christianity, spent some time as a missionary to the Frisians (Holland) and also endowed a monastery in Mercia. Wilfred also acquired huge wealth and was a combination of cleric and speculative nobleman.

One of the reasons for the continuing dispute was a decision in 677AD. to break up the huge Northumberland diocese into three bishoprics, York, Ripon and a new centre for a new bishop based in Lindsey.

The Lindsey diocese continued despite the capture of the province by Aethelred of Mercia in 678AD. This ended over 40 years of peace during which Conisbrough's Minster church was built in Northumberland style. Conisbrough was never again to come under Northumbrian control.

The See of Lindsey continued until the Viking occupation, and the bishop's names that have survived are Ethelwin, Edgar and Cynibert who was bishop at the time of Bede, 730 AD. We know that Lindsay was represented at an assembly called by the king of Mercia at nearby Austerfield in 702AD. It is named at a further assembly in 737AD. when thirteen diocese were present.

There is evidence just outside St. Peter's, Conisbrough, of a standing cross. During the time of Theodore such crosses were erected where daily prayers were said if a church was not present. Sites which became popular usually became the site of a church. Conisbrough's cross would be one of the places were Paulinus would stand and preach, (628 to 633AD).

During the 7th and into the early part of the 8th century England progressed into a more orderly society, but a "totally united English kingdom" was still far away.

Bede felt this keenly and tells us that the kingdom of Mercia "held sway" over all provinces south of the River Humber. One such, Offa (757-796,) was the most powerful English king before Alfred the Great. Offa's Bretwaldship (overkingship) now encompassed virtually all the area we now call England. It is highly probable that he would have visited the fortifications along the River Don at some time and, if so, would have called at Conisbrough.

There are few documents written in Offa's time that have survived to the present day, but one is a south Saxon charter which shows Ealdfrith, King of Lindsey, in Offa's company when it was signed. This is the only evidence to show that Lindsey still had its own king, presumably a subordinate to Offa. Conisbrough at this time was part of Lindsey.

By 720 several north European towns were developing into commercial centres and had begun to inter-trade. Several foreign traders had a presence at York (Ebor). This commerce would have required treaties and agreements to be made, and through such arrangements the Vikings would be aware of the situation in this country.

In 789 the first war ships of the Danes came to England. This Viking landing was a minor affair. The "sea borne pagans" were plundering Lindisfarne in 793, Jarrow in 794 and Iona in 795. England had not suffered a foreign attack for two centuries and the desecration of three of the most holy places caused great outrage. It was a further generation before the nuisance raids of the Viking developed more serious overtones. The large raid on Kent in 835 began three decades of almost yearly incursions, ending with the arrival of a full scale invading army.

The word Viking, coined by their victims, means "foot piracy" and involved both Norwegians and Danes. They were far from being total barbarians, but as the population of their countries grew it became very hard to make a living there. They heard stories of fertile lands with monasteries full of easy plunder, and began to make raids. It is surprising that the earlier raids were not followed sooner.

In 829 Egbert, King of Wessex, conquered Mercia and all that was south of the Humber. He made incursions into Northumberland and Wales, both of which submitted to him and paid tribute. Geoffrey of Monmouth tells us that "Conans Burgh" with all of Hengist's treasure was taken by King Ambrosius and that King Egbert came here after he subdued the northern part of Wales, suggesting a date of 830AD. Egbert's final years were spent dealing with the Danish invaders in the south and west of his kingdom. He was a remarkable man and managed to live well into his 60's. When he died in 839 he had reigned 37 years and 7 months and is normally called " the first King of all England ".

In 854 the Danish royal dynasty fell, and after that the raiders increased in great numbers. They seem to have used two main routes, one around the north of Scotland to the Western Isles, the other southward to the east and south coasts of England and onto France.

Hence the raids and settlements in Ireland, Scotland, Wales and Cornwall were mainly Norwegian (by the northerly route), while those in England and France were mainly Danish (by the easterly route).

In 866 the Danes entered Northumbria and occupied York. Conisbrough also became part of the Viking dominion and the influence of the Danes is well marked in this locality by place names.

Denaby means:-Village of the Danes; Cadeby means:-Kati's farmstead and Micklebring means:-The Great Slope.

Before the arrival of the Vikings there would have been a very small settlement on the opposite bank of the Don were the river was crossed. In times of conflict this could be abandoned and a retreat made to the main fort. Opposite the Mexbrough fort is where "Old Denaby" is now situated and the Vikings took this place as their own. Old Denaby began to be used as the name for the original Denaby when the colliery company built houses for the miners near Denaby Main.

Alfred The Great To The Norman Conquest

King Alfred the Great did not have dominion over this area. Conisbrough is within the lands remaining under Danish (Viking) influence as a result of peace terms settled after Alfred's resounding victory at Chippenham in May 878.

It was King Edmund (The Magnificent), Alfred's warrior grandson, who captured many towns from the Danes, including the boroughs Leicester, Lincoln, Nottingham, Derby and Stamford. By 920 the Northern boundary of Edmund's kingdom was along the fortifications protecting the crossing places of the River Don. Amongst these were Templeborough, Masborough, Mexborough, Conisbrough and Sprotborough.

Conisbrough was once again part of England, now within the kingdom of Wessex. The strategic position of Conisbrough must have made it a vital point in Edmund's defence system. He brought all of Northumbria into subjection in 940.

Very little is known about the Saxon Fort. It was probably built to enclose the existing church- today's village centre, or, on a spur of limestone that was capped with clay- the site where the castle now is.

The earliest authenticated reference to Conisbrough is contained in the will of a Saxon lord named Wulfric Spott, who was a trusted minister of King Ethelred, "Ethelred the Unready". The will was executed about the year 1000AD and disposed of possessions at "Dunecastre" and "Conningesburg", the latter being bequeathed to his nephew Elhelm. From Elhelm, Conisbrough passed into the hands of Earl Goodwin of Wessex, and from him to his son Harold, who became king for a short time (January to October 1066).

King Edward (The Confessor) reigned 1042-1066. This accession was largely contrived by Earl Goodwin of Wessex, the most powerful man in England at that time. Edward married Earl Goodwin's daughter Edith in 1045 but the marriage was in name only for all Edward's inclinations were directed towards a religious life. He had Westminster Abbey built but matters of government were left in the hands of Earl Goodwin and his able son Harold.

When King Edward died (5th January 1066), Harold, who by now had succeeded his father, was chosen king. The threat of an invasion by William of Normandy came very early in his reign, and Harold maintained his army in a state of readiness on the Isle of Wight for about four months. From February to May the comet we now know as "Halley's comet" was seen over England. This did not help Harold, as superstition held that this was a portent of a great happening to come.

In September Harold received news that his brother Tosteg, who had long been exiled, had landed in Yorkshire with Harold Hardrada, King of Norway and a large army. The northern Earls, Edwin of Yorkshire (whose lands included all villages north of the River Don, and Denaby, Hooton Roberts and land towards Rotherham south of the Don) and Morcar of Northumberland with the men of their Earldoms, were required to contain this invasion until reinforcements could arrive.

For the decisive battle they chose a site on the left bank of the Ouse near the village of Gate Fulford two miles south of York. For the greater part of a hard day's fighting they barred the only road, but their lines eventually gave way and large numbers of their men were cut down or drowned.

This gave Harold time to force-march the regular army northwards, calling at Conisbrough and the surrounding area, which he owned, to collect reinforcements and stores. Harold inflicted a crushing defeat on the Norwegians and others at Stamford Bridge on the 25th of September 1066.

For many years prior to 1066 Harold had maintained a mistress, Edith Swan-neck, who had borne him many children, but in 1065, aged about 45 years, he had made a political marriage with Ealdygarth, widow of the King of Gwyneth and Powys (Wales). She had at least one son to Harold by this marriage, who was also named Harold, but his fate is unknown. It can be assumed that Harold would have kept his wife with him at court in Winchester and would have sent his mistress and children to one of his other estates. The furthest was Conisbrough, so this would have been a likely choice.

A Tentative Reconstruction of St. Peter's, Consibrough c.1066AD

The Battle Of Hastings And The Norman Conquest

News arrived of William's landing on the south coast on the 29th of September. Harold had had little time to have his wounded attended to and the dead buried following the the battle of Stamford Bridge.

Before leaving Yorkshire Harold would have called all his Housecurls (professional men at arms) from all the forts along the Don, and as many of the Fyrd (militia) that could make the rapid 260 mile return march south, which was done on horseback or stout pony.

Conisbrough and the rest of the manor would have been drained of all its able men, only the wounded, old and very young would be left behind.

Hastings was a hard-fought battle, and on the 14th of October 1066, Harold fell. Tradition maintains that his eye was pierced by an arrow, but careful examination of the battle scene as depicted in the Bayeux Tapestry shows the figure of Harold being felled by a sword blow, and it is a nearby soldier who has the arrow in his eye.

From the Norman Conquest the history of Conisbrough is fairly clear, although we possess no evidence which proves conclusively which of its owners was responsible for the erection of either the curtain wall or the castle keep.

In 1053, William, Duke of Normandy, made an advantageous marriage to Matilda, the daughter of his neighbour, Count Baldwin of Flounders. There was some ecclesiastical objection to the marriage, the reasons for which have never been clear. It has been said that she had had a liaison with a Flemish commoner named Gherbod, and that two of her children were to him. They were Gherbod, who later received the Earldom of Chester, and Gundred who married William de Warenne.

William and Matilda became devoted to each other in an age where marital infidelity was the norm. William's marriage may well have been partly motivated by his growing ambition to gain the throne of England, for Matilda was a direct descendant of Alfred the Great. William was first cousin once removed from Edward the Confessor.

The events were to show that although the Battle of Hastings had decided the fate of the nation, its significance only appeared slowly.

The northern earls had provided no contingents at Hastings, and the spirit of London was unbroken. William now had an army of less than 6,000 men, but he proved himself to be a wise general, and instead of seeking another major confrontation inland he went along the south coast, and as he progressed the ports surrendered on demand. At Winchester, through the influence of Edith, the Confessor's widow (Harold's sister), the city surrendered, but William returned it to her as a dowry.

Having secured the coast he then encircled London. During this time leading English nobility came of their own will and swore allegiance to him. Eventually Edgar Aetheling, the last male heir of the Cerdic line, along with the northern earls, Edwin and Morcar, a number of Bishops and leading men of the City of London submitted before William, who, in his turn, promised to be a good Lord to them.

On Christmas Day 1066 William was crowned at Westminster Abbey. England had now had three kings within one year. Although the south and east of England quickly submitted to William's rule, there were risings in various parts of the country over the next five years with the west finally submitting in 1068.

Earl Edwin had made his peace with William before Christmas 1066, but he had left the court disappointed because the king had not given one of his daughters in marriage to him. Up to the end of 1068 William left the north region to its own government by local magistrates and overlords. The Earls Edwin and Morcar led a rebellion which was put down by William in person in 1069. Edwin was killed through treachery of his own followers while escaping to Scotland.

Conisbrough would have been visited at this time and whoever King Harold had left to run his estate would have had to make their peace with William, or fight.

William the Conqueror personally made settlements on matters relating to the great families of the land. He would have been familiarised with his predecessor's relationships. We know that both English and Norman wives ran their husband's estates when they were absent. William was not all bad, and the many English landlords who submitted to him survived with their wealth and status intact, but if they revolted against him, it was said he was stern beyond measure.

The estate known as "The Great Feast of Conisbrough" was managed by an English person after 1066, and must have pleased the Conqueror because it was not razed to the ground as all other estates around it were when the "Harrying of the North" took place in 1069.

At this time Denaby was not part of the living of Conisbrough, it was part of a manor which incorporated Hooton Roberts and Newhill, and so suffered greatly at this time.

The operations of 1069-70 ("Harrying of the North") were distinguished from ordinary warfare as they were a deliberate attempt to ruin the population of the rebellious estates by systematic destruction, carried out by professional soldiers under the close personal supervision of a ruthless and badly-frightened king.

Although William believed he had subdued the northern rebels, in autumn 1069 he came close to losing everything he had spent years fighting for. The English arose in revolt almost everywhere at once but the main troubles were in the north of the country. William's troops in the garrisons at Durham and York were massacred and the towns burnt and looted, while a Danish war fleet sailed into the River Humber.

When William eventually got to York he set out to avenge his losses by deploying troops to destroy everything for miles, food, household goods and buildings were destroyed, farm animals slaughtered, and any of the population caught were killed. About 100,000 people perished as a result. This was a purely revengeful action, as no gain was made by king or soldiers.

The area affected was Shropshire, Cheshire, Staffordshire, the west of Nottinghamshire and Lincolnshire, Derbyshire, Yorkshire and Durham to the Tyne.

By about 1086 order had returned, England was more peaceful than any other place in Christendom, and it was said that a man could journey in safety with his bosom full of gold the length and breadth of the kingdom. Justice was dispensed according to the best of the old laws with suitable reforms. Those who failed to meet the king's standards were removed from office and punished.

The legal position of an ordinary villager is not easy to determine. The evidence suggests he was still personally free within the bounds of his lords manor, and by a combination of paying rent and either estate or military service, he could maintain his land holdings as he had done before the Conquest.

The Warennes

King William had in his court, and kept close to his presence, a small group of Earls. These were closely interrelated with each other by descent or marriage, and one such was Earl William de Warenne.

The Warennes held a small estate in the south-west of Normandy at a place called Mortemer. How they came into the court of William, Duke of Normandy, is not known, but their relationship had developed to almost permanent companionship around the time of the invasion plans, and continued throughout their lives.

William de Warenne, to 1089

William de Warenne, one of William's chief helpers, greatly distinguished himself at the Battle of Hastings, and as a reward for his services was granted,
(i):-the Rape of Lewis, which had two castles, Lewes and Reigate, and over a hundred manors.
(ii):-in Norfolk, Castle Acre, and with it, 145 manors. This seat was to become his and his heir's favourite residence.
(iii):-in Yorkshire, the Great Feast of Conisbrough, which, although only defined as one manor, encompassed 22 other places over a great area, and was therefore quite a substantial holding.

He had by now married Gundreda, the Conqueror's daughter. In 1088, when in his sixties, he was created Earl of Surrey and given the manor of Wakefield for quelling an insurrection against William the Second. He died in the following year and was succeeded by his son William.

William, Second Earl de Warenne, 1089-1138

William, the second Norman owner of Conisbrough, endowed the Priory of Lewes (Sussex) with the churches of Harthill, Dinnington, Braithwell, Hatfield, Fishlake, Sandall, and Conisbrough.
During the 50 years he held the title his loyalty was often tested by the quarrels between the kings and their families. He died in 1138 succeeded by his son, also named William.

William, Third Earl de Warenne, 1138-1148,

At the Battle of Lincoln in 1146 he fled the field. King Stephen was captured there, and William left England to join St.Bernard's second crusade to Palestine. He died on the return journey, about 1148. Seven sons predeceased him and he left an only daughter, Isabel, who first married the fourth son of King Stephen, - Prince William de Blois.

Prince William de Blois, Fourth Earl de Warenne, 1148-1165,

Prince William was only nine years old when he took the De Warenne titles by his marriage to Isabel. He made no active contribution to the history of Conisbrough being pre-occupied by his large estates in Europe. He died without issue.

The Anglo–Norman realm 1066–1154

Hamelin Plantagenet, Fifth Earl De Warenne, 1165-1201,

As the widow of an Earl, Isabel became the King's ward, and he, (Henry II) selected his half brother, Hamelin Plantagenet, a natural son of Geoffrey of Anjou, as her second husband. Lord Lyttleton, who devoted the latter years of his life to his "History of Henry II", says:- "Any man who Isabel now took in marriage would receive the Earldom of Surrey, with all the other honours and possessions of her father in England and Normandy. Possessions so great, that without alarming the jealousy of the crown, they could not have been added to the wealth of any other noble family, especially as the lady to whom they had descended was very closely related in blood to the Kings of France and Scotland". It was therefore not only from affection for his brother, but from the maxims of good policy and reasons of state, that Henry interested himself in promoting this marriage".

The marriage probably took place in 1165, and so highly did Hamelin regard the honour, he relinquished his father's coat of arms and adopted those of Isabel. We gather some idea of the extent of his possessions from particulars given in a schedule according to feudal law drawn up when Henry, in the 12th year of his reign, and on the occasion of his daughter's marriage, certified that Hameline held 60 knights' fees.

He was present at the coronation of Richard the First, (Richard the Lionheart) and was one of the treasurers of the fund raised to provide Richard's ransom when he was detained by the Duke of Austria. His personal contribution being 340 pounds, which was a considerable sum in those days.

It is the actual events of this era which were to become the basis for the works of later novelists who mixed these facts with romanticised fiction to create the well known legends of Robin Hood and Ivanhoe.

It is to Hamelin that the erection of the keep of Conisbrough Castle is generally attributed. Before his time there is no distinct historical reference to any castle here, whereas in his time we find several. The first is contained in a charter of endowment of a chapel. "Hamelin and his wife, Countess

Isabel, with the favour and assent of their son William, give in pure and perpetual alms to God and to St Mary, Mother of our Lord, and to the holy Apostles Philip and James, and to the chapel of the same Apostles, which is seated in the Castle of Conisbrough; 50 shillings yearly to be received off the mills of the manor of the said town: for the love of God, for the health of their souls and for the health of King Henry, his Lord and brother". This appears to be a first endowment and not an augmentation of an endowment already existing.

During excavations at the castle an altar stone was discovered. This has five consecration crosses and a niche for a small relic box, (where parts of a saint would have been kept). This altar stone is now kept in the memorial chapel within St. Peter's church.

King John came to Conisbrough to visit his ageing uncle Hamelin Plantagenet in 1201.

William, Sixth Earl de Warenne, 1201-1239

It is now assumed that he constructed the curtain walls of the castle.

William fought the French in Normandy with King John. All the Normandy estates, including those of the Warenne's, were lost when the King was expelled from France by Philip Augustus.

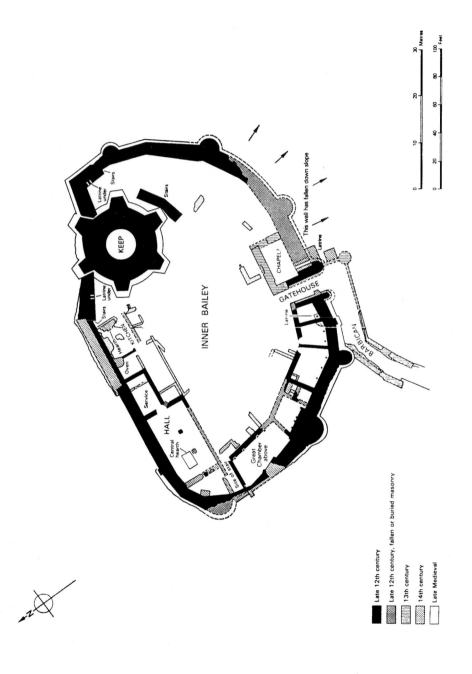

KEEP

INNER BAILEY

Latrine under Stairs

Stairs

This wall has fallen down slope

CHAPEL?

Latrine

GATEHOUSE

Latrine under

Stairs

KITCHEN

Hearth

Oven

Service

Latrine

BARBICAN

HALL

Central hearth

Site of stair

Great Chamber above

N

Metres
Feet

Late 12th century

Late 12th century, fallen or buried masonry

13th century

14th century

Late Medieval

27

John, Seventh Earl de Warenne, 1239-1304

The seventh Earl was only 5 years old at his father's death, so his mother, Maud, took custody of the castle and lived out her days there. At 12, John was married to a sister of Henry the Third. He was on this King's side at the Battle of Lewes in 1264, where Henry was taken prisoner by Simon de Montfort. De Warenne fled to France and his estates were confiscated. He returned however, and again took the King's cause in the Battle of Evesham in 1265. De Montfort was slain and John's estates were restored to him.

When this Earl was asked, in the reign of Edward I, under the famous "Quo Warranto" statute, to prove his title to his lands and honours, he drew from its scabbard, an old rusty sword and exclaimed, "Here is my warrant, my ancestors came with William the Bastard and conquered these lands with the sword and with the sword I will defend them !".

When his right to own a gallows at Conisbrough was challenged, he stoutly maintained that it was a privilege conferred by William the Conqueror on William, First Earl de Warenne, and the right had been exercised subsequently by all his ancestors.

That executions took place here is proven by a record given in the Hundred Rolls of the Wapentake of Strafforth, wherein the jury, after due investigation of a complaint of high-handed action on the part of the Constable of Conisbrough Castle, found as follows:- "They (the jury) say that Nigel Drury, constable of the castle of Conisbrough, seized in the town of Rotherham, a stone of wool from a certain chest which belonged to a certain woman, who was hung at Conisbrough, and carried off the said wool against the inhibition of the bailiffs of Rotherham". It will be noticed that no comment was made regarding the legality of the execution of the woman, but only of the forcible seizure of the property which had belonged to her.

The 7th Earl had a son and a daughter. His daughter married John Baliol, King of Scotland. His son was accidentally killed at a tournament held at Croydon in Surrey, the title passing to his grandson who eventually succeeded as 8th Earl in 1304.

John, Eighth Earl de Warenne, 1304-1347,

John, 8th Earl de Warenne, was a famous warrior, and as a reward for his military services in Scotland he was granted the Castle and Honour of Peak

28

in Derbyshire. In 1317 he abducted Alice de Lacy, wife of the Earl of Lancaster from Pontefract Castle and took her to his own Castle at Reigate in Surrey. Lancaster divorced his wife and then laid siege to John's Yorkshire castles of Sandal and Conisbrough. On the 13th of November 1317, Edward the Second issued a writ commanding Lancaster to cease all warlike operations. He obeyed, but held the manor of Wakefield and the castle of Conisbrough until he was executed for treason in 1322 at Pontefract.

Edward the Second made a brief stay at Conisbrough in November that year. During this stay he ordered repairs to be made to the walls and main gate of the castle. In 1326 De Warenne regained possession of his northern estates.

The will of John, Eighth and last Earl de Warenne, was dated from Conisbrough Castle and therein describes himself as John, Earls de Warenne, Surrey and Strathern, Lord of Bromfield and Yale. He died on the 30th of June 1347, leaving no legitimate issue and therefore his estates reverted to the King.

House Of York

Edmund de Langley, Lord of Conisbrough 1347-1402

On the 6th of August 1347, King Edward the Third issued at Reading, "Letters Patent", conferring the Castle and lands of Conisbrough on his fifth son, Edmund de Langley, a boy of six years old. He was afterwards created Earl of Cambridge, and later, the first Duke of York. His tenancy of the castle lasted until 1401 and it is to this period that the majority of the improvements to the accommodation of the inner ward most probably belong.

His eldest son Edward, Duke of Albemarle, succeeded in 1402.

His younger son, having been born at Conisbrough was known as Richard de Conisbrough, later Earl of Cambridge.

Edward, Duke of Albemarle, Second Duke of York, Lord of Conisbrough 1402-1415

Edward succeeded his father as Duke of York, but fell at the Battle of Agincourt in the year 1415 without issue.

He had married Maud, who continued to live at Conisbrough until her death in 1446. The succession now passed to Maud because Edward's natural heir, his younger brother, Richard de Conisbrough, Earl of Cambridge, had been executed for conspiracy against the King earlier in 1415. This is described by Shakespeare in Henry V, Act II Scene II.

Richard de Conisbrough had married Anne Mortimer, daughter of Roger, Earl of March, whose mother was the daughter and heiress of Lionel, Duke of Clarence. The later claim of the House of York to the throne was reliant upon this marriage. The eldest son, Richard was to become the Third Duke of York, and enter into possession of the Castle and Manor of Conisbrough.

1415-1446. The succession remained with Maud until her death, the title then passed to her nephew Richard.

Richard de Conisbrough, Third Duke of York, 1446-1460

At the Battle of Wakefield, 24th of December 1460, both he and his eldest son were killed. Therefore his second son, Edward Earl of March, succeeded him, and in 1461 ascended the throne of England as Edward the Fourth, the first Yorkist king. (His fourth son, Richard, was to usurp Edward V, one of the "Babes in the Tower").

Edward, Earl of March, King Edward the Fourth 1460-1483

Edward usurped his third cousin Henry VI to become King. At this time and throughout the War of the Roses (1450-1485), Conisbrough was a Yorkist stronghold.

On Edward IV's death in 1483, he was succeeded by his infant son, who would have been crowned King Edward the Fifth.

King Edward the fifth, 9th April to 25th June 1483

Thirteen year old Edward was kept with his younger brother, Richard of York, in the Tower of London, they both disappeared from there in suspicious circumstances. They have become known historically as "The Babes in the Tower".

This event is attributed to Richard, Duke of Gloucester, who usurped the throne to become King Richard the Third in June 1483.

The record of these events was written in the time of Henry VII who actually had more reason than Richard to dispose of these two brothers.

Richard the Third, 1483-1485

Richard, Duke of Gloucester, was the fourth and only surviving son of Richard, Third Duke of York. He was able to usurp the throne by taking advantage of the infancy of his nephews.

The Battle of Bosworth Field which took place on August the 22nd 1485 brought to an end the "Wars of the Roses". Richard III and a large part of the Yorkist army including men from Conisbrough, were killed.

Conisbrough Castle was never garrisoned after this battle and it was allowed to fall into disrepair. The victor at Bosworth Field, Henry Tudor, became Henry the Seventh.

The Decline Of The Castle

To the Tudors.

Conisbrough was now once again the private property of a king, and when Elizabeth, daughter of Edward IV, married Henry VII, Parliament declared that Conisbrough Castle was to be forever annexed to the Crown.

At what period Conisbrough Castle was allowed to fall into decay is a moot question. The fabric of the castle would have suffered considerably during the siege and capture by the Earl of Lancaster. The integrity of the structure would be first threatened if repairs to make it habitable were only carried out to a minimum standard to save money. Over the following years this would weaken not only the structure but also the will to carry out routine repairs as they became necessary elsewhere in the castle. The earliest evidence of this is the collapse of the main wall from the gatehouse eastwards past the chapel for about 30 metres.

Support is lent to this contention by an order issued by Lancaster during his brief occupation of Conisbrough, 1319-1322, to his keeper of the woods of Conisbrough to supply timber for the repair of the roof of the chapel. This cannot have been the chapel in the keep, since its roof is of stone. For the everyday use of the garrison there was a second chapel in the inner yard and it is a fair assumption that this would be the chapel that received damage during the siege. In November 1322 after Lancaster had been executed, King Edward the Second visited the castle and ordered repairs to be made to the walls and main gate.

The decline seems to have accelerated during the Tudor period, when most benefits to be derived from occupancy of the castle or associated estates were nullified or re-allocated. In 1522 Sir Henry Wyatt and John Melton were bailiff and steward respectively of the "Lordship of Conysborowe". Doorwards and Constables of the Castle were still in office.

A report of 1538 during the reign of Henry the Eighth indicates that the process of ruin was fairly advanced. Leland, a Kings Commissioner, in an account of his itinerary writes: "From Tikil to Conisbrough is 4 miles by a stony way and enclosed ground, where I saw no notable thing but the Castle standing on a rocket of stone and ditched. The walls of it hath been very strong and full of towers"

His omission to mention the Church is not surprising as such a building was outside the scope of his task. The commission, given under the Great Seal, was to "examine the REMAINS of ancient buildings and monuments".

The castle remained in royal hands throughout the Tudor period until it was bestowed by Queen Elizabeth (1558-1603) upon her cousin, Henry Carey, Baron Hunsdon. He was the son of Mary the older married sister of Henry VIII's second wife Anne Boleyn. In May 1997 the American Society of Geneolagists, revisionists of Tudor History, was stating that Catherine and Henry Carey were bastard children from an affair that Henry VIII and Mary had from 1522-26

The Civil War.

The castles of Sheffield, Tickhill, Sandal and Pontefract played an active part during the struggle between Charles the First and the Parliament, and in 1646 Parliament ordered these to be dismantled.

No evidence exists to show that Conisbrough Castle played any part in the quarrel, this is probably the reason why it is not mentioned in that order and that so much of the keep and walls remain.

During the war the castle remained in the Carey family. Mary Carey, the last of that name to own the Manor of Conisbrough, married a gentleman of Norfolk named Coke.

It remained in the Coke family until 1737, when the Castle and Manor were purchased for the sum of 22,500 pounds by the fourth Duke of Leeds, then resident at Kiveton.

The nineteenth and twentieth centuries

In 1801 a writer in the "Gentleman's Magazine" gives an account of a visit he had just paid to Conisbrough Castle. In which he expresses the hope " that the building may be more respected", by which it is probable that he wishes to convey that the castle was being allowed to deteriorate and being used as an easily available supply of building stone by the villagers. Many of the stone-built houses and walls constructed in Conisbrough at this time, of which some remain to this day, contain stone which was quarried and shaped in Norman times and which formerly formed part of the curtain wall or the buildings within it.

A Doctor Hunter, writing in 1828, mentions the presence of a slight fissure in the interior wall of the keep. This is a natural deterioration caused by water ingress rather than subsidence due to local coal mining as has been claimed in later times.

Sackville George Lane Fox, the 12th Baron Conyers, acquired the castle from the Duke of Leeds in 1859. It remained with this family until 1920.

It is unfortunate that none of these latter owners cared sufficiently for the castle to carry out any repairs or maintenance.

The ownership of the castle passed to Conisbrough Urban District Council for a nominal sum and it has remained in the guardianship of the nation since 1949.

Over the last 50 years considerable sums of money have been spent trying to rectify over 500 years of neglect.

The Birth Of A Village

The whole of the United Kingdom has seen dramatic changes in population.

With the exception of the Domesday Book 1087, there was never a full census until the nineteenth century.

Before the Roman conquest, when the Celts had control over the whole of what is now the United Kingdom, the population was thought to be about 500,000. At the height of the Roman conquest it is probable that the population of England alone had reached 2 million. However, by Saxon times, 700AD, it had fallen back to around 500,000 due to 200 years of war, famine, plague and disease.

The Conisbrough area in Roman times was comprised of isolated farms in wood clearings. When it became a fortified village it would have needed a population about 150 to make a viable community.

No chronicles have survived from this period about Conisbrough.

In times of war the related surrounding area would have sought refuge within the fortifications, and it is probable that this would have increased their number to around 250 people. With this increase it would have been possible to defend the area against all but an organised army. This would have been the situation when the Vikings came, around 841.

From the records of other places where the Vikings attacked we know their main interest was plunder, but that some communities were allowed to buy peace. Eventually they became interested in settling and brought their families with them.

Here it is probable that the Vikings would have been forced to negotiate a peace treaty rather than suffer large losses trying to overcome the fort. We know the areas in which the Vikings settled locally from place names in the surrounding area. Examples are described in an earlier chapter.

Alfred the Great became King of Wessex and all England in 848. He had many skirmishes with the Vikings and eventually had a great victory in May 878, but was never able to evict them. In his peace settlement he agreed that they could have the land north of the old Roman road, Watling Street, (the A5), which runs in an arc from London to Chester.

Conisbrough was part of Danes Law for about 90 years until it was retaken by Alfred the Great's warrior grandson Edmund the Magnificent in the year 920.

At the heart of each early district was a Royal Moot House and Hall. Each modern county contains several such places, usually with names that give a clue, e.g. Kingston, Kings Lynn, Bury St.Edmunds, other names have been corrupted to some degree over the years and are now less obvious e.g. Conisbrough (one of the popular suggested origins being "Conan's Burgh"), Petersfield, Salisbury, Basildon.

The local subjects would come to one of these places to pay their taxes and rents. The amounts due were derived from a complex system of assessment. Land was reckoned in "hides" each notionally the area needed to support a free peasant. Hides were grouped in multiples of twenty (a score). Not all farmers were "free", and manpower on a demesne lord's estates may have been by slaves.

Alfred also laid the foundations by which England was to be administrated. He divided it into counties that survived virtually unchanged until 1974. Each county was subdivided into parts known as "Hundreds", but in the north, which had been occupied by the Danes, the name is "Wappentakes". Conisbrough and Denaby were in the Wappentake of Strafforth.

The record regarding Conisbrough in the Domesday Book (1086 AD) is as follows:-

"In Coningesburg Earl Harold had 5 "carucates" (A carucate was the amount of land which was capable of being turned over by one plough in a year, and was generally reckoned at 120 acres) of land to be taxed. There is land to 5 ploughs. William de Warenne has now 5 ploughs in the demesne, there are 21 villains (tenant farmers) and 11 borders (labourers and smallholders) between them having 11 ploughs. There is a Church and a priest, and two mills worth 32 shillings. Wood pasture one mile long and one broad. To this manor belonged 28 villages included in the Great Fee of Conisbrough".

The Domesday record is silent with regard to any owner's residence at Conisbrough, and yet it can be inferred from a clause in the foundation charter of Lewes Priory that one existed. William de Warenne, at whose cost the Priory was built, stipulated that the monks were to provide entertainment for him when he travelled between his Norman possessions and his estates in Yorkshire, and his only possession at the time in the north was the Great Fee of Conisbrough.

One could speculate that the reason for the book's reticence on the subject

Left: Castle from Low Road Coronation Park.
Right: North wall of nave laid in Northumbrian style inside St Peter's church.

Left: Madonna and Child in Porch of St Peter's Church (Saxon).
Right: Holywell in a deprecated state for the last 20 years. Sheffield Road.

Left: St Peter's church site used for worship for over 1,300 years,
Right: Wellgate residents collected their water from here upto 1909.

Above: General view of Cadeby Colliery. Loaned by Gerard McLister.

Above: Denaby & Cadeby Miners Memorial Chapel.

Above: Old Hall Church Street probably 17th century has been a private shool, village post office and church curators home, now converted into a restaurant.

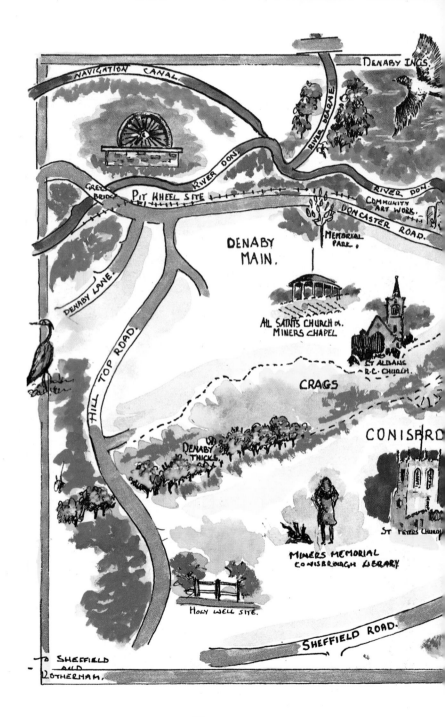

NAVIGATION CANAL.

DENABY INGS.

RIVER DEARNE

RIVER DON.

RIVER DON.

GREN BRIDGE

PIT WHEEL SITE

COMMUNITY ART WORK.

DONCASTER ROAD.

DENABY MAIN.

MEMORIAL PARK.

DENABY LANE.

ALL SAINTS CHURCH & MINERS CHAPEL

ST ALBANS R.C. CHURCH.

HILL TOP ROAD.

CRAGS

CONISBRO

DENABY THICKS.

ST PETERS CHURCH

MINERS MEMORIAL
CONISBROUGH LIBRARY.

HOLY WELL SITE.

SHEFFIELD ROAD.

TO SHEFFIELD
AND
ROTHERHAM.

40

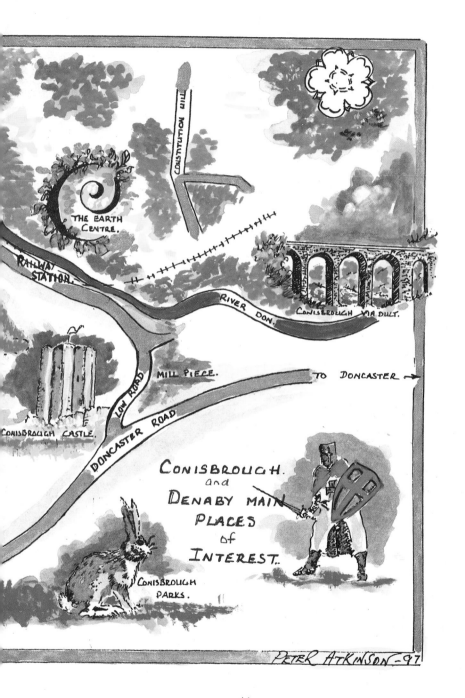

THE EARTH CENTRE.

CONSTITUTION HILL

RAILWAY STATION.

RIVER DON.

CONISBROUGH VIADULT.

MILL PIECE.

LOW ROAD

TO DONCASTER →

CONISBROUGH CASTLE.

DONCASTER ROAD

CONISBROUGH.
and
DENABY MAIN
PLACES
of
INTEREST.

CONISBROUGH PARKS.

PETER ATKINSON -97

41

Above: Tree planted in the Memorial Park, Denaby in memory of Dunblane victims by the Primary School children and Cllr Dorothy Layton Mayor of Doncaster.

Left: Spring time, Doncaster Road, Denaby with the Reresby Arms in the background.
Right: Jonathan Smales Chief Executive of the Earth Centre on site with the "Friends".

Above: Ex colliery wheel in memorial chapel.

Above: March for peace and jobs at Swinton. The last occasion that Cadeby Miners marched behind the NUM branch banner. Loaned by Gerard McLister

Above: Conisbrough Castle built by Hameline Plantagenet 1180 AD.

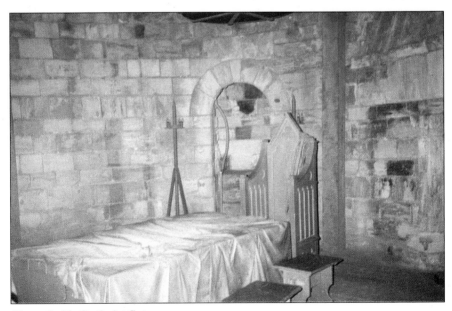

Above: Inside Castle 1st floor.

of the management of the manor of Conisbrough is due to the private arrangement that King Harold would have made if, as we believe, he had left his mistress and children here. William the Conqueror would have probably confirmed these arrangements and would not have required the details to be revealed.

Domesday's record of Denaby states:-

"In Newhill, Hooton Roberts and Denaby, Wulfheah, Ulfkil (and) Ulfkil had 6 carucates of land to geld where there could have been 4 ploughs. Roger now has one plough, there are 6 villains and 6 borders, and the site of a mill, woodland and pastures a furlong long and 2 broad".

The Domesday book was ordered by the king in 1087 so that he could have some record of his holdings in England. These were far greater than anything he held in Normandy. His income from his new holdings, over 13,000 pounds per year, was greater than any other king in Europe. A hundred pounds per year was sufficient to sustain a baron with a castle and estate.

The devastation in the "Harrowing of the North" is clearly shown in the records of the doomsday book,

pre-conquest rent values in Yorkshire were 3479 pounds from 1782 villages
       in 1086 rent values in Yorkshire were 1169 pounds from 988 villages
which shows a 66 percent drop in income.

After the rebellion in 1069 Earl Edwin forfeited all his lands to William who gave them to Roger de Bully, one of the barons who was with him at Hastings.

Domesday records that Earl Edwin had a hall at Laughton-en-le-Morthen, this manor had eight villages, with 23 spokesmen, 15 villains, 17 borders.

This manor's revenues fell from 24 to 15 pounds.

Roger de Bully also acquired 43 other villages north of the Don including Mexbrough, part of Edwin's former estates.

In the Mexborough area revenues had fallen from 6 to 2 pounds
In Newhill, Hooton Roberts and Denaby they had fallen from 4 pounds to 1.50 pounds.

Male population of Yorkshire 1068.

Freemen	Spokesmen	Villains	Borders	Cottate	Priests	Others	TOTAL
58	448	5033	1806	16	136	78	7570

This shows a very sparse population, the whole of Yorkshire being no greater than just a small town of today. Also note the absence of figures for the female population which indicates the beginning of an era in which the status of women fell. Up to this time women could generally hold titles and inherit and bequeath with equality to their male counterparts.

There were no slaves recorded in Yorkshire, but in the rest of the country the figure was about 10 percent

A freeman was a person with independent means that was not reliant on land ownings, e.g. a knight or merchant

A spokesman enjoyed many privileges, he was relieved of many of the burdens and tied duties of the ordinary villager.

A peasant could gain his freedom by escaping to a town where, if he remained unclaimed for a year and a day, he became free.

A man or woman could marry outside their normal place in the class structure with their lord's permission. This created some movement, upwards or downwards depending on the circumstances and favour of the lord.

Although the local lord could impose his will on his subjects he in turn was subject to a higher protocol via overlords to the king who had unquestionable authority. The Magna Carta (1216) imposed limitations on the arbitrary power of the Crown and was a practical assertion of existing law and custom as applied to the nobility.

By 1202 Conisbrough's population had grown sufficient to sustain a market in the village. There is no certain evidence of its location in the modern street pattern, although was a village green at one time, situated at the junction of Church Street and High Street.

In 1289 the market was relocated to the neighbouring village of Braithwell, which was part of the honour of Conisbrough at that time.

As a result of extremely hot and dry summers in the years 1320 and 1321 the harvests were so bad that a population fall of about 15 percent occurred, mainly due to starvation. This is the most likely origin of a local legend which tells of the arrival a holy man shortly after all the existing wells and streams had dried up. Following a service in the church he led the villagers, singing and dancing in procession, down Beech Hill where he cut a wand or rod, then continued along for a little way, stopping where a steeper section of the ground meets a gentler slope. The Holy Man struck the ground with the rod he had chosen and fresh water erupted from the ground showering the villagers. Water still runs from "Holy Well" to this day. It further justifies the title "Holy Well" because it does not dry up or freeze over. The oldest maps clearly show it as "Holy Well", with the ground behind called Holywell Hill.

When, in 1348/9, England was devastated by the Black Death (Bubonic Plague), some country areas suffered less than the large towns. This was attributed to particular wells in those localities and so began the tradition of "Well Dressing" as a thanksgiving. The reformation period saw an end to most of these ceremonies, but in many parts of Derbyshire however the tradition survived and continues.

In 1379, according to the Poll Tax records, there were 78 households, each of which paid an average of 4 pence in tax. Craftsmen and gentlemen paid higher rates of tax. For instance, there was a potter, a Franklin (landowner) called De Westby, a swineherd and a cartwright, who each paid 3 shillings and 4 pence.

Throughout the rest of the middle ages Conisbrough remained a large village rather than developing into a town, as during this time the Royal Lords were pre-occupied, firstly with the "100 years War" with France and then the "War of the Roses", and so neglected their northern estates.

Parkland covered almost half the area of Conisbrough and it was used as a hunting ground by the nobility. Conisbrough Park (which included Parks Farm, Conisbrough Lodge and Birk Lodge) was of Anglo Saxon and Danish origin. This park and Sheffield Manor were the only parks in South Yorkshire.

The old village had now developed its present form with a Moot Hall on the site of the present Church Hall, and with the house and cottage now known as "The Old Hall,(Cromwells Restaurant)" nearby.

The increase in population continued at only a modest pace from now until the "industrial age" was firmly established elsewhere in Yorkshire.

Although we are fortunate to have burial registers which began in July 1555, and baptism and marriage registers from January 1559, no specific population figures were written.

In 1801 Conisbrough was a large agricultural village with a population of 843. Most of the old limestone buildings near the church date from the time when farmers, agricultural labourers and rural tradesmen formed the largest part of the community. There were millers, tanners, saddlers, sawyers, boot and shoe makers and wheelwrights, making it very self-sufficient. At this time there was not a single brick building in the village, they were all of limestone construction.

47

Industrialisation And Population, Their Growth.

During the 1400's there were opencast coal workings in Denaby Fields and two watermills in Conisbrough:- one at the Mill Piece (near the Memorial Garden) and the other at Burcroft. These continued in use right up to modern times.

In 1575 farm timber was sold locally for 1900 pounds. A document of 1656 shows that the woods were leased to Thomas Bosville Pagdin Wilson. Gervais Boseville owned Conisbrough Lodge at that time and part of the park was leased as agricultural land.

Pottery making at the kilns at Firsby, a hamlet between Conisbrough and Ravenfield, had by now grown into an important local industry. This was due to the availability nearby of good quality clay and coal.

On the completion of the Don Navigation Company canal the waterside at Burcroft attracted new industries. They came for ease of commercial transport rather than to make use of the water as mill power. Waterways were cheaper, faster and much easier to use than the roads of the day.

In 1777 the Walker family of Masborough, Rotherham, iron founders and lead refiners, owned land in Burcroft near the River Don, containing houses, stables and a shop.

In 1779 they constructed a new boring mill there for the boring of cannon, and it was here that those used in the Napoleonic Wars were prepared.

By 1805 the mill had passed to John and Thomas Mullins, who as forge masters, began to produce scythes, sickles, hooks and other agricultural implements. They were succeeded by William Linley.

In 1847 Thomas Booth and his sons Thomas and George took over. George began running the firm in 1869 and held the business until Rawding, Blackburn and Rawding bought it in 1898. They retained the name of Booth, and successfully exported their tools to all parts of Africa, Asia and the Pacific. Eventually Spear and Jackson took over the firm and made all kinds of edge tools until the closure of the works in 1976.

In Marchgate, formerly known as Codder Alley, stood the old tannery, of which some of the buildings are still in existence. Tanning was an important industry in the community, for furnishing horse saddles, reins and even uniforms for soldiers during the Napoleonic Wars.

New Hill was constructed in 1766 to improve access to the village, a study of Old Hill will illustrate the vast improvement the new road provided in its time.

Main roads, financed by tolls, were beginning to be considerably improved. What we now know as Doncaster/Sheffield Road, the A630, was a new Turnpike in 1787. The wider roads recorded in Conisbrough at this time were Northcliffe Hill Road, Kearsley Field Road, Highfield Road, Montague Road and Broomfield Road. Lesser roads were Mill Road and Drake Head Road. Low Road was constructed in 1774 to improve access to the Burcroft area.

In 1795 the population of Conisbrough was 840

Railways were first built for the transportation of coal from the mines being developed elsewhere in South Yorkshire. In the 1840's the South Yorkshire Coal Railway was constructed from Doncaster to Barnsley, via Conisbrough and Denaby. In 1850 when the Great Northern Railway from Doncaster to King's Cross was inaugurated, it enabled West Riding goods to be sent speedily south.

The Kilner Brothers started their glass bottle manufacturing business at Castleford in the 1830's. In 1840 Caleb Kilner founded the works at Thornhill Lees, near Dewsbury, and then established the Conisbrough factory in the 1850's. The site was eminently suitable for the manufacture and distribution of glassware due to its proximity to the new transport facilities. In the 1881 census, Caleb Kilner is listed as being a glass manufacturer employing 171 men, 33 women and girls, 109 youths and boys, many of whom came from the Castleford and Thornhill Lees area. Jars for preserves and pickles were made as well as bottles for medicines, cordials, wines and spirits. The most famous product was the "Kilner Preserving Jar" which is still produced today under license. They opened a distribution centre in Blundell Street, North London and won many international gold medals for the quality of their products which were exported to most parts of the world. The firm ceased trading about 1937 when George Kilner of Ivanhoe Lodge was managing director.

As the 19th century progressed, so did the industry in the outlying parts of the village. The firm of Lockwood, Blagden and Kemp for instance, leased two stone quarries and two lime kilns at Levitt Hag, (a short distance along the river towards Doncaster), from the Wrightson family for 600 pounds per year rental.

Thomas Simpson lived at Ashfield House and was a brick and tile maker who also manufactured sanitary pipe ware up to the end of the 19th century.

In 1857, at the time of the Conisbrough Enclosure Awards, there were 1,840 acres of land in the township and 200 acres in Conisbrough Parks. The Lord of the Manor was Mr. Lane Fox. Priory Manor House was owned by Mr Pitt Rivers.

The population of Conisbrough in 1861 was 1,665.

The population of Denaby in 1861 was 203

A brickyard and quarry was established in 1860 on the west side of Clifton Hill. The good quality clay found there was used for the making of facing bricks. In the 1930's 200,000 bricks per week were produced. In the 1950's the quality of the clay deteriorated so only "commons" were made until production ceased in 1961. The site was used during the second world war as an army transport depot. The quarry part has now been used for landfill and the remainder as a maintenance and storage depot for a large self-drive vehicle hire company.

Denaby had a pottery between 1864 and 1870 where a form of management and worker co-operative was tried. This was the first of its type in the pottery industry.

The sinking of coal mines began at Denaby in 1863 and Cadeby in 1889, the extraction of coal began in 1867 at Denaby Main. It was both the most easterly and deepest mine in England at that time.

The need for accommodation for the large number of mineworkers and their associated needs led to the formation of the industrial village of Denaby Main. This "Model Village" which had approximately 49 houses to the acre was the work of Messrs. Pope and Pearson, colliery owners, who leased the land from the Fullerton Estate. J.B.Pope had previously raised money to build the Hull and Barnsley railway line.

Although it might have been anticipated that the population of Conisbrough's would increase with these events, infact it did not. There are two likely reasons for this, the first is that the easily built land close to the

50

existing village was already occupied, including some farms, the second is that by populating Mexborough instead they had easy access to further employment prospects, eg. Manvers and Kilnhurst mines, glassworks and brickworks locally.

It is interesting to note that until this time Conisbrough was the predominant village and would have been expected to develop into a town. However Mexboroughs population, which had been about half of Conisbrough's, grew at a spectacular rate for 50 years and then doubled that of Conisbrough which remained mainly agricultural.

The population of Conisbrough in 1871 was 2,107

The population in Denaby was 1,467

There were two licensed breweries in Conisbrough: Nicholson's, opposite the end of Holywell Lane, and Ogley's at Hill Top. They supplied the local inns and taverns, but beer was also brewed and sold from houses and cottages in the village. In 1822 the landlord of the Eagle and Child was John Smith and, at the Star, Edward Goodacre. The Star Hotel burned down in 1911 but was rebuilt almost on the same site. In 1836 there are two more inns recorded: The Red Lion situated at the top of West Street, and the Hill Top Inn, owned by the Ogley family, where Earl Fitzwilliam met with horse and hounds in the hunting season.

The Railway Inn, so called because of its patronage by early railway and viaduct workers, is now known as the Castle Inn.

Even with the advent of industry, farming remained important here until the time of the First World War. Many farm labourers were employed under the hiring system and there was a statute fair at Conisbrough as late as 1870.

Denaby Powder Works opened in 1889, it was one of the four companies which founded Imperial Chemical Industries (I.C.I.). During the first world war 10-inch shells and 3-inch trench bombs were being filled and sent by rail to the war fronts. When the works closed in 1963 it was employing about 200 people making electric detonators.

The town continued its growth into the 20th century with the expansion of coal mining, stone quarrying, wood turning, sweet manufacturing, metal working, gas manufacture and leather working.

The population of Conisbrough in 1901 was 8652.

The population in Denaby was 2670.

Coal Mining And The Community To The Late 20th Century

The Industrial Revolution brought a huge demand for power to drive the increasingly complex machinery being invented and developed. The use of natural sources (wind and water) for the great manufacturing mills had been quickly exploited to its maximum. The invention of more efficient steam power meant that factories were no longer restricted to being built near water courses. The opening of more mines to feed the hungry steam engines brought huge population increases to many small towns and villages. It soon became obvious that it would be more economic to establish the users of the power near to the source, hence a wide variety of industry scrambled for land and workers near to the mines. This caused yet another great population drift as people followed the opportunity of relatively secure and well paid work.

The establishing of the two immediately local collieries has already been described. The 20th century had an inauspicious beginning with a very bitter miners strike in 1902-1903. This became known as "The Bag Muck" strike when miners and their families were evicted from their homes. This was to be the last time that employers were allowed to evict strikers from tied homes.

Local collieries were caught up in the "National Strike for minimum wages" in March 1912. It involved three quarters of a million men throughout the industry and resulted in victory for the miners after 40 days. Due to the lack of maintenance of the workings, coal could not be got from Cadeby for several days after the return to work.

On the 9th of July 1912 Cadeby Colliery was rocked by a terrific explosion, 35 of 37 men working in the south district were killed. The combined rescue teams of Denaby and Cadeby collieries, a number of pit management and government inspectors, including H.M. Divisional Inspector of Mines, W.H.Pickering (said to be one of the leading authorities on coalmining at the time) were then caught in a second explosion, this brought the immediate death toll to 75, this rose later when men succumbed to their injuries.

An estimated crowd of 80,000 gathered to await the news of further rescue work. Their Majesties, King George V and Queen Mary, who were staying in the area on a short tour and had visited Conisbrough the previous day, came to the mine accompanied by Earl Fitzwilliam and Lord Stanfordham.

The General Strike of 1926 brought the miners to the forefront once again. They were eventually forced to accept lower rates of pay.

In 1932 the No.2 shaft at Denaby Main was deepened to the Silkstone and Parkgate seams. Pit Head baths were built in 1938 but the building was commandeered and used as a factory producing tools for the armaments industry during the Second World War. The baths were re-opened for miners in 1948.

In 1947 all local collieries became part of the "National Coal Board". Denaby Colliery closed in its own right in 1968 with the workforce transferring to Cadeby Colliery. Demolition and site clearance was not completed until 1987.

Cadeby miners were at the forefront of the conflicts during the the strikes in 1972, 1974 and 1984/5.

The workforce was gradually run down by voluntary redundancies and transfers until production was ended in late 1986. The demolition was carried out in 1987 and the site landscaped in 1988.

Education

It is recorded that up to 1540 there was a Grammar School in Conisbrough. Children of influential parents were given some schooling, it was never free, and the quality was questionable. Working class parents found it very difficult to pay for their children's education therefore very few of their children received any schooling.

In Conisbrough, in the mid 1800's, there was a private school situated at the Old Hall, Church Street which accommodated about 16 boys, and was run by the Reverend Ellershaw.

In 1873 the first board school was established in Conisbrough, this was a result of the Education Act of 1870.

This important reform was passed by Gladstone's first government, and set up school boards which built schools for children up to the age of 13 years old if there was not an existing church school.

In the 1890s schooling became state funded and it became compulsory for all children to attend school up to the age of 13. Parents who did not send their children to school regularly were prosecuted.

In Conisbrough and Denaby schools were built to accommodate all children. Within 20 years, Station Road, Morley Place, Balby Street and Rossington Street Schools were built. The latter erected in 1893 by the colliery company incorporated a large hall which could be used by the villagers out of school times. Many famous singers and bands performed in concerts and dances here.

In 1926 the Roman Catholic Church built its own school, St Albans.

In 1929 a Middle School called Northcliffe was opened, it was purposely built to accommodate the older children and had special classrooms so that subjects such as woodwork, metalwork, science, cooking, needlework and physical education could be taught. Boys and girls were segregated until it became a Comprehensive school.

No further schools were built until Rowena Infants in 1953.

In recent years replacement schools for Balby Street, Rossington Street and Morley Place have been constructed.

Two completely new schools have also been provided, Ivanhoe School and the Athelstane School for special needs have been built.

Fullerton Hospital, opened in 1905 at a cost of 3,000 pounds on land donated by J.C.H. Fullerton and supported by mineworkers contributions, closed in 1989 and is now a special needs school taking day pupils and boarders.

Housing In The 20th Century

In Conisbrough gas began to be installed for lighting from 1870, and the first building to be "switched on" was the Red Lion Hotel. Water mains were laid from 1903 and gradually replaced the wells.

In Denaby, gas supplied by the colliery company was usually laid to the houses as they were built. Water to the houses began to be installed from 1902.

Like the colliery workers, so the glassworkers had to be housed near to their place of employment. Starting in 1895 houses were built opposite the factory in Denaby, between the railway and the road. The streets were named after the Kilner brothers, John,William and George, and the origins of the business Thornhill (Street) Lees (Terrace). When these were fully occupied they built at Low Road, New Conisbrough, and on Burcroft Hill. These were all completed before 1914.

The late 1920s saw the start of the exploitation of a further coal seam at Cadeby Colliery. A large increase in the workforce was needed, and so to attract miners from afar, and to house them and service their needs, the Conanby "Avenues" estate was built. Several social features were included, for example a shopping parade, public house, doctor's surgery and accommodation, midwife/nurse's bungalow, welfare/community hall, sports ground and grassed communal areas. The influence of the mine owners and investors can be seen in the Avenue names i.e. Barnsley and Parkgate:-coal seams, Denaby and Cadeby:-collieries, Fitzwilliam, Halifax, Montague, Chambers and Pope:-major investors, landowners, benefactors and directors.

In 1935 Denaby Amalgamated Collieries were employing 6,000 men, but generally unemployment was high, particularly bad years being 1929 and 1931. In an effort to relieve this the Government offered inducements for councils to carry out public works. In Conisbrough this resulted in slum clearance schemes, namely;-

Mount Pleasant (Sheffield Road), Dale View, Beech Hill, New Hill, Marchgate, Kent Yard and Wellgate. Also at this time the Priory Manor, an ancient building, was demolished.

In both villages the council started to to build the first "Council Houses" where unemployed men, in some cases having been out of work for years, were given 12 weeks paid labour on site in the years 1936 to 1940. The Daylands Avenue estate and Church Road in Denaby are typical examples.

The availability of Government money enabled the mine owners to renovate their properties in Denaby and Conanby between 1938 and 1940. A total of a quarter of a million pounds was spent on this work.

In 1946 the Council continued to have housing built, in fields adjacent to Conanby. The winter of 1946/47 proved to be one of the severest on record, with large snow falls over several weeks.

One of the strategies of the National Government during the war in anticipation of an acute shortage of skilled workers was to set up Technical Colleges where practical as well as academic skills were taught. Mexborough Schofield Technical College was one of these, and one of the courses taught was pre-building. The course ended at Easter so those newly trained could seek work in the finer weather. Unfortunately the Easter of 1947 was still in the grip of the severe winter weather. This class had no prospects of employment so an agreement was reached between the Urban District Council and Ben Bailey to take on these 15 to 16 year old. They built 12 houses in a 2 year period under the builders supervision, during this time they were free to take up any permanent opportunities that occurred in their preferred trade. The quality of their works makes it impossible to distinguish these houses from those built alongside by regular tradesmen.

The Oval was originally laid out to receive factory-made pre-fabricated bungalow's. These were immensely popular because of their fitted kitchens with appliances.

The Windmill estate, another council development, was built in the early 1950's

The Groves estate, made to house miners displaced from mainly Durham mines, was built in the late fifties by the National Coal Board Estates Office. It is so called from the names given to almost all the streets being derived from the "name of a tree or shrub":-Grove. Up to this time most estate street names had been taken from public figures, land and mine owners/managers or historical figures and legends.

In Denaby in 1962 the Urban District Council put forward plans to demolish and replace 1,700 old dwellings. A start was made in 1964 when Thrybergh Terrace was demolished, but the scheme did not gain real momentum until the early 1970s. The project was taken over by Doncaster Metropolitan Borough Council in 1974. By 1984 708 new houses were built.

In the last 30 years, along with the national trend towards home ownership and latterly the government embargo on Council funded building, there have been considerable private and Housing Association developments and infills locally.

Religion

The habit of regular church-going started to change in the 18th. century. It had been the tradition of hundreds of years for people from all walks of life to go to church every Sunday.

Country people had become distant from the Church of England because of having to pay Tythes, a form of taxation on crop returns paid to the church for the upkeep of the vicar who had often become more affluent than themselves. In Conisbrough the Reverend Watkins was complaining that the locals were unwilling to tell him about their crop returns in 1801. The tythe barn where one tenth of the local produce was to be collected was situated where the Police Station now stands.

About this time John Wesley, a disillusioned Church of England minister who was considered a great preacher and hymn writer had started preaching his own style of religion. In Conisbrough there were sufficient converts by 1810 to warrant the establishing of a small chapel. This was situated in Crow Lane (Castle Terrace). In 1876 they built a new substantial chapel with a magnificent gallery and rostrum. These were the work of a local craftsman, Joseph Appleyard.

The Baptist Chapel started in the mid 19th. century in a room at the bottom of New Hill. It moved to a tin hut on its present site in the late 19th. century. This was subsequently replaced by the present brick building. Its large hall has been used for many social functions and was used as a hall and dining room for Morley Place School before it was relocated.

In Denaby the growth in population with diverse beliefs led to the establishment of:-

1891-Epworth Hall Methodist Chapel. In 1924 it was altered and a mission hall plus school room added. Worship ended in 1974. This is now the processing laboratory of Ellif Photography.

1893-The Salvation Army met in Rossington Street School until its Citadel was built in 1928. It was subsequently refurbished in 1985.

1895-Primitive Methodist Chapel, changed to Lowfield Methodist Chapel in 1932 upon the amalgamation of all Methodists. This chapel was closed in 1968. It is now used for commercial purposes.

1902-A Baptist Chapel was opened on Doncaster Road. This closed in 1920. The building was taken over and became the Denaby and Cadeby Colliery's Official's Club in 1922. It was acquired by the members in 1988 and is currently a private club.

St. Albans Roman Catholic Church

Built on an acre of ground, a gift from Andrew Montague, the building took a year to complete in 1898 and cost 4,000 pounds. The one bell, named "Mara Immaculate" was positioned in a newly built tower in 1910.

Monsignor Donal Bambury the present priest, holds a unique distinction, being made a Freeman of Doncaster in 1995 for his work in the parish.

The Parish Church of Denaby Main.

St. Chads church was created from a farm barn, at the same time as other farm buildings were cleared to make way for the Reresby Arms Hotel. The church was used from 1891 until 1920 for worship, then as a sunday school and Scout headquarters until 1930. It was ultimately demolished in 1932 to make a car park for the Reresby Arms.

St. Chads had a Mission in Blyth Street, built with a wooden frame covered by corrugated sheeting. It was opened in 1912 and had a Sunday School. It was renovated in 1951 but demolished in 1964.

All Saints parish church cost 3,500 pounds to build in 1900, the land being a further donation from Andrew Montague.

Denaby and Cadeby Collierys held the patronage and living for many years. It was demolished and a new building erected across the road in 1975. Some of the material from the old church was re-used in the new. It was the only parish church to be built in the Sheffield Diocese for 30 years.

This new building was badly damaged by fire in 1977, being repaired then rededicated by 1979. Adjacent to the church is the purpose-built Miners Memorial Chapel built in 1989 from bricks salvaged from Cadeby Colliery. It is the only one of its type in the country, with much of the work done by volunteers and a quantity of the materials were donated.

Under a mahogany Holy Table, having glass sides to protect it, is a one ton piece of coal mined at Manvers Main.

There is also half of one of the winding wheels from Cadeby Colliery along with other mining memorabilia.

The Cenopath In Coronation Park, Low Road, Conisbrough

59

Saint Alban's Roman Catholic Church, Denaby. Opened in 1898.

The new Church of All Saints, Denaby within it Miner's Memorial Chapel

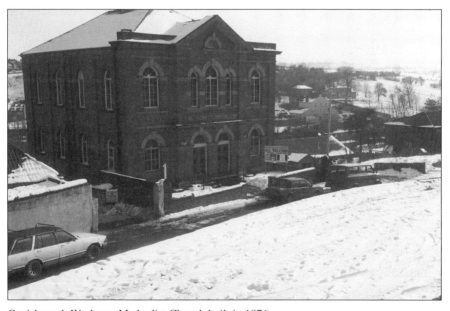

Conisbrough Wesleyan Methodist Chapel, built in 1876

One of the last stone buildings in Church Street

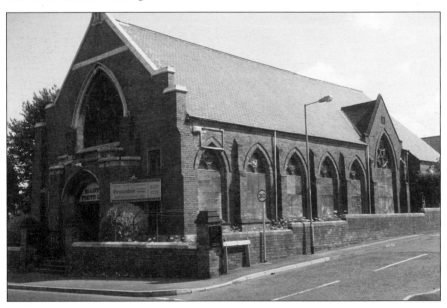

Epworth Hall Methodist Chapel, Built in 1891. Worship ended in 1974.
Ellif Photography closed in May 1997

Miners Memorial. Old Road Conisbrough in memory of the hundreds of men and boys who lost their lives. The Price of Coal

Wheel Memorial to the 203 men and boys who lost their lives at Denaby Colliery near the site of the pit, Doncaster Road

Community Art Works, Doncater Road across the road from Denaby Main Hotel

Rossington Street Old School erected by the Colliery Company in 1893 which incorporated a large hall.

Priory High Street built 1807 several owners over the years, used as a convalescent home for poor children. During the Second World War was used as civil defence purposes. Now used as offices by the Borough Council.

Police Station stands where the Tithe Barn was. In the middle is the formerly vicarage.

Looking from the "Crags" to where the "Earth Centre" is been built on the old Cadeby Collery Colliery site.

St. Peter's Church, Conisbrough

One of the great mysteries of Conisbrough is "When was the building of St. Peter's Church started ?".

When standing in the nave, look at the north side wall, which is on the left hand side when facing the altar; it tells much of the early history. A wall of stone of this type of construction, i.e. arches supporting a substantial main wall would have had to have been built principally as it now stands. It would not be possible to build this type of solid stone wall and then cut out and add the arches later, (even with today's technology and machinery), as has been suggested in early publications.

There are three arches of Roman influence, supported by two short round pillars, each with a base moulding and carved capitals. The pillar nearest the altar is of Roman influence, whilst the one furthest from the altar is of Irish (Celtic) influence.

The wall above the arches is stone laid in the "Irish-Northumberland" manner. In good light it is possible to see the outline of three windows which have been subsequently been stoned up. The one towards the rear of the church, near the crown of the arch, is of the "round-headed" Celtic type and is original to the wall. The author has seen this type of window only in Northumbrian or Irish churches built before 700 AD. There are three similar windows in St. Pauls church at Jarrow, the church that Bede used.

The two nearest the existing windows are of late Saxon type, they would have been added after 920 AD when it is assumed the church roof was altered. They would have been placed to admit more natural light when glass became more readily available. As is obvious, they were later filled in and the present, even larger, windows fitted.

The wall would have been the work of at least two masons trained in differing schools, one Irish trained, the other of continental craft. This would suggest the wall was built no earlier than 634 AD, but no later than 10 years after the Synod of Whitby (which was in in 664 AD), after which all the Irish bishops had returned home with the bulk of their followers.

It is probable that Aiden himself or one of his senior missionaries would have come to Conisbrough to oversee the building work and thus introduce the Celtic influence to the architecture.

A wall of this type, with the inclusion of arches requiring great skill, time and expense, would not have been built without purpose. This suggests that there would have been either a side aisle or veranda leading to other essential parts of a complex, e.g. dormitory, refectory.

This supports the belief that St. Peter's was a "Minster Church", i.e. one staffed by monks, and part of a collection of buildings within an enclosure, sometimes linked to a farm. Minsters were always associated with the centre of a royal estate. St. Peter's is possibly the only example of an aisled Saxon parish church in the north of England.

Whilst still in the nave, but now looking towards the altar and upwards, it is possible to perceive the profile of the original roof. The pitch indicates that the original covering would have been thatch.

All the other buildings in the area; houses, barns, storehouses, and workshops would have been constructed with wooden frames infilled with walls of small stones laid in cow dung and lime, or wattle panels daubed with mud to keep wind and rain out. Either type would usually have a thatched roof.

Mention is made in the Doomsday Book of a church and priest at Conisbrough, but the earliest named priest found to date is Guy Rufus 1165-1202.

In 1486, with Henry VII's marriage to Elizabeth of York, Conisbrough reverted once again to Crown property.

There was a grammar school here up to 1540.

During Henry VIII's reign an English translation of The Bible was placed in every church. To ensure that it had to be read in the church it was usually chained to a teaching desk.

We do not know how the priests at St. Peter's would have been reconciled with the closing of the monasteries between 1536-39 and the repeated changes of doctrine between Protestant and Catholicism. During this period many churches had their Holy images (pictures or statues) removed or destroyed by the Protestant reformists. In St. Peter's however it was the later Victorian restoration which caused their loss. In 1549 the Archbishop of Canterbury, Thomas Cranmer, put together the first Book of Common Prayer for all clergymen to use. Following a ban lasting about 300 years priests were again permitted to marry. Over the years they became generally more affluent than the local farmers and tradesmen.

ST. PETER'S CHURCH, CONISBROUGH

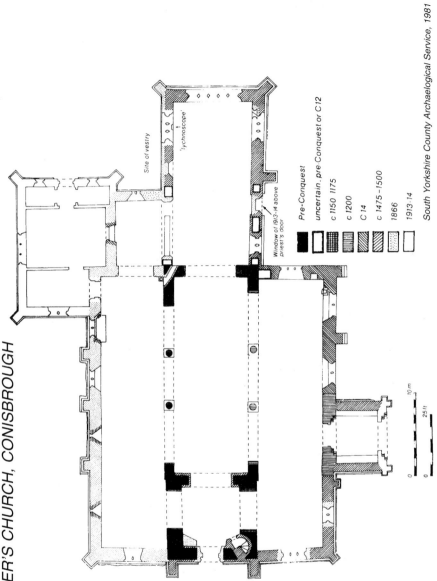

Site of vestry

'lychnoscope'

Window of 1913-14 above
priest's door

Pre-Conquest

uncertain. pre Conquest or C12

c 1150 1175

c 1200

C14

c 1475 - 1500

1866

1913-14

South Yorkshire County Archaelogical Service, 1981

0   10 m

0   25 ft

St. Peter's Church Today

The present building, which has undergone many restorations and enlargements, embodies the remains of a Minster church built around 640AD.

As built and up to the Norman Conquest the building appears to have consisted of a nave with an aisle to the north side and a porch, possibly with flanking chambers, on the south side. The chancel was much smaller than its present size. A small tower was built after the Viking occupation.

In the latter part of the 12th. century the Saxon building was remodelled, the porch and lateral chambers being replaced by three bay aisles.

The Tower

The original western structure built around 940 was a tower or a two storey porch, similar to Ledsham church. The projecting stones which now form the string course would have carried a floor or roof plate which was later removed when the tower was heightened.

In the 12th. century the tower was considerably extended and remodelled. It has semi-circular arches opening into the aisles. The windows above the arches are different in character from other 12th. century work in the church and are the earlier stonework incorporated in the upward extension.

In a corner is a door for the spiral stair turret leading up to the belfry. The church clock, donated in memory of Simeon Simpson was installed in 1882. The earlier set of three bells was replaced by a peal of 8 bells in 1914.

The Porch

The outer arch of the porch is a 15th. century copy of a 13th. century model. There is a 15th. century slab bearing an inscription for which no translation has yet been found. Directly above is a relief carving built into the wall, this depicts a seated Maddona and child beneath a shouldered arch. A similar one is in the porch of the pre-conquest church at Breedon-on-the-Hill.

The South Aisle

As it now stands, the south aisle is late 12th. century. The doorway is the much restored original to that work.

ST PETER'S CHURCH, CONISBROUGH
INTERNAL ELEVATION OF NORTH WALLS OF NAVE AND TOWER

0 _____ 5 metres

SOUTH YORKSHIRE COUNTY ARCHAEOLOGY SERVICE

Pride of place is given to an elaborate stone tomb chest lid dated c.1140-1160 which was found in the churchyard. The top bears a series of medallions enclosing mounted fighting knights, winged beasts and signs of the Zodiac. One side has a warrior fighting an impressive dragon, and a bishop with crozier stands behind him.

This would obviously be for a person of great standing. Could it have been for a descendant of King Harold and his mistress, Edith Swan-neck, embroiled in the struggles of the day between Saxon and Norman kingships as later depicted by Sir Walter Scott in his Ivanhoe novel?

Nearby is a tapered coffin lid with relief carvings of two birds. It has suffered a good deal of damage and has proved difficult to date.

Behind this lid is a 14th. century Piscina and Aumbry.

The east wall window arch is 14th. century work although much of the tracery has been replaced.

There is also a fragment of the shaft of a stone cross which has been dated as late 10th. century.

The Nave

The nave is tall and narrow with relatively thin walls. The stones of the north wall are laid in Northumbrian style (knobbled stone laid irregularly), and are clues which helped us to date the original structure - later medieval walls are of dressed stone, with regular courses and are thicker. Walking forward from the door, facing the north wall, it is possible to see the outer corners of the original church.

As you walk into the centre of the nave the blocked remains of three windows can be seen on the north wall, the two outer ones are square whilst the more central one is round-headed and is placed opposite the porch of the original building to light the entrance. These windows were blocked in turn when the nave walls were progressively heightened, the last filled being in the 15th. century when the present windows above the aisle roofs were inserted.

Part of the 13th. century nave roof survives, with some remnants of carved decoration on the tie beam above the chancel arch.

In the Norman period the nave was to be enlarged, as this work was to take some years to complete it was achieved by:-

(i)   A new south wall was built outside the existing solid wall.

(ii) The wall around the chancel arch was heightened and widened.

(iii) The North wall was extended upwards.

(iv) A new roof was then placed over the existing one while the old roof and south wall were demolished.

The church could have continued in use during much of this work.

The North Aisle

This aisle was widened in 1866, its walls being totally rebuilt. Although carried out in the 19th. century the work is a copy of an earlier style, probably late 12th. century, two windows of that era have been reset in the west part of the wall.

In the south-east corner is a pillar Piscina with a square bowl, used for carrying away the water used for rinsing chalices. Above it is the opening for a "squint" cut through the wall across the corner of the chancel to give a view of the communion table. This would be used by lepers or others excluded from the congregation as a means of taking part in the services, or at least seeing the altar lights (hence the term Lychnoscope).

A brass plate at the rear of the tomb recess in the north wall bears an inscription commemorating the founder of a chancel here, Nicholas Bosville, who died in 1523.

There also is a medieval cross slab grave cover of a fairly conventional type.

The Font

This is of the 15th. century and probably dates from the remodelling of the church in that period. The west face of the bowl bears a figure of Christ seated, and the east face depicts the resurrection.

The Chancel

The chancel was originally almost square in shape but the 15th. century saw the chancel enlarged by extending eastwards. The evidence for this is:-
(i) the change of masonry in the north wall.
(ii) the original position of the communion table can be deduced by peering through the lychnoscpe (squint) from the north aisle.

There is some 15th. century glass, including pieces depicting 'Our Lady of Pity' and Prior Atwell of Lewes. These are in a window in the south wall.

Many of the chancel's ancient features (e.g. wall paintings) were destroyed in the 'restoration' carried out in the Victorian (1837-1901) era. At this time the north aisle was rebuilt and an organ chamber added to the north side of the chancel.

The recently blocked up doorway covers an early 'Priest's Doorway' which can be seen more clearly from the outside.

The old iron grid on the left of the communion table is a low side window through which the priest could view the chancel from the vestry.

The Memorial Chapel

This was an organ chamber from 1866 but the organ was taken out in an unrepairable condition in 1954. It is believed that parts off it were used to repair the organs of other churches. The chamber was refurbished and converted into a memorial chapel to honour the dead of the Second World War.

In this chapel is the altar stone from the chapel endowed in 1189, by Hamelin and Isabella, in the inner bailey of the castle. This was discovered in the early 1970's

Recreation

Denaby

Football. Denaby United Football Club first played in the Midland league in 1902 on a site behind the Reresby Arms. They moved to the Tickhill Square ground in 1912.

Open Air Swimming Pool, Denaby - the Parish Council, with the help of the colliery company, built an open air pool in 1910. The pool cost 310 pounds, it was closed and filled in in 1930. It was situated near the present football ground.

A detachment of the Territorial Army (KOYLI's) was founded in 1908, a club and drill hall being built the following year. It continued through both World Wars but was closed in 1960. The building, on Doncaster Road, has since been used as a supermarket and wholesale warehouse.

Denaby Comrades Club opened in Rossington Street in 1919 for ex-servicemen, and was renamed the British Legion Club in 1924. It had a bowling green and rifle club. It was originally a corrugated tin hut, but was replaced by a brick building, which closed in 1983. Denaby Memorial Park cost 2,000 pounds, Construction started in 1931 and it opened the following year, the two and a half acre site being donated by Capt. J.F.O.Montague. The cenotaph was commissioned by Conisbrough Urban District Council and cost 249 pounds and 15 shillings. It was dedicated on the 8th. of November 1953, and was unveiled by C.J.Picket M.B.E., M.C.

The Empire Picture House opened in 1913 and closed as a cinema in 1963. It has subsequently been used as a bingo hall, a snooker club and gymnasium.

Annerley Street Institute opened in 1886, it was enlarged in 1898 to contain reading, recreation and billiard rooms. It had a library of 1,400 books, and was supported by subscription, the colliery proprietors and others. It closed and the building was demolished as a part the re-development programme in the 1970's.

The St. John Ambulance Brigade Headquarters, better known as the Blood and Bandage, was built in 1909. In its time it had a brass band, a nursing division and cadets. It was closed in 1970 and demolished along with nearby houses in Cliff View. The brigade was disbanded in 1984.

The Cricket Club was founded in 1888, it moved to its new ground in 1900. A timber pavilion was erected in 1901, which was replaced by the present brick structure in 1924. The playing area was levelled in 1910. In the 1920's and 30's a number of athletic events took place here with several well known celebrities taking part. The proceeds from these events went towards the hostpital funds.

The tennis club was founded in 1907 having two hard courts off Tickhill Street, it ceased in 1970.

A bowls club was founded in 1909. A second green was added in 1920 and a third in 1935. The present green was laid and new pavilion built in 1968.

Denaby and Cadeby Miners Welfare was built in 1922. Two years later the Welfare Committee had the present swimming baths built. They were refurbished in the 1980's and are still in regular use.

A Scout group existed in Denaby before the First World War. They moved into a purpose built hut in Bolton Street in the 1920's.

The founding of the Tom Hill Youth Club was discussed before the Second World War, but it was 1949 before a building was erected. In 1966 the present centre was opened with a five-a-side football pitch built next to it.

St.Albans Club was built by 100 persons paying one pound per brick. Alterations were carried out in 1963 when a lounge and games room were added.

The Recreation Ground (swing park) opened in 1929 and was used until the late 60's. It was lavishly equipped and reputed to be the finest in the area. It boasted a shop and a full time attendant. Despite being a very progressive amenity it never had proper toilet facilities provided. The site was then used as a landfill site in 1972. It was levelled and made into a football field in 1984.

The library was built and opened in 1964 to replace a ground floor room in the Miners Welfare building.

Conisbrough

Coronation Park opened in 1911 to commemorate the coronation of George the Fifth. It was a gift from Mrs. Godfrey Walker, and cost 600 pounds. In the park is the cenotaph to commemorate the dead of the two World Wars. In one corner there is a fountain with lantern above. The village stocks have been re-sited here after being rescued through the endeavours of a former well known resident of Conisbrough.

The Mill Piece, Low Road is mentioned in the Doomsday Book. In the 1920's and 30's it was used as a boating lake. In recent times much restoration work has been carried out here.

Conisbrough picture house opened in 1912 and closed in 1959. The building was then demolished and a, visually out of character, parade of modern shops built. The site, in Church Street, mainly comprises the Cooperative supermarket.

Northcliffe Hill (Crag's) is one of the last limestone crags to remain undeveloped in the area. At the present time Doncaster M.B.C. in liaison with Denaby Gateway Forum are carrying out improvements costing over 400,000 pounds to improve access and amenities of the site.

Conisbrough Library is now on the site of the original Morley Place School. It has had several locations including two shops in West Street, an old stone building across from the Baptist Chapel on Old Road, and also near the Methodist Chapel.

There were a number of Scout groups in Conisbrough with differing religious associations - Methodist and C.of E. In recent years they have amalgamated and use "The Forge", a conversion of an 18th. century barn located on Beech Hill/March Street. There is still a Guides and Brownies Pack associated with the Methodist Chapel. There is also a Guides and Brownies Pack which in recent times meets at the Ivanhoe School.

The Ever Changing Present

In the last 30 years Denaby has been almost totally rebuilt. The pit company houses were cleared away by demolition then renewed to an improved standard and layout. There are new shops, including two supermarkets, and industry has been attracted to purpose built trading estates.

However, Conisbrough in the last 50 years has a poor record of looking after its surviving stone buildings and village character, both of historical importance. Most of the new buildings in the village pay scant regard to maintaining the village heritage, and are totally out of character with hundreds of years of settlement.

After the 1984 miners strike and the closure of all local collieries, the peoples of both villages suffered the loss of thousands of job opportunities. This area suffers mass unemployment, reaching over 33% at times, with only remote Northern Ireland districts, in civil conflict, being worse.

Young people leaving school are unable to find sustainable work. There is no quick fix to this situation which is exacerbated by the ideallogical clash between local and national government policies. There has been help from the European Economic Community and the British Government, but even with adequate investment it would take many years to return the district to near its former prosperity.

A number of small groups of people in the area are working on schemes to help the recovery. In Denaby there is the Ivanhoe Trust and The Forum. In Conisbrough, the Highway Centre has been established and also the Conisbrough and Denaby Development Trust.

The criteria for securing funds for the day-to-day running of all the agencies involved are continually changing, and with the Dearne City Challenge ending March 1997 further problems are envisaged.

All endings present the opportunity of a new beginning. Let us hope that from now we can take the philosophy of the International Rio Conference of 1991, particularly agenda 21, (the taking into full account of the aspirations of the local people in decision making) as the cornerstone of policies to mould our future.

Towards The Future, The New Millennium.

External events change so fast that it is virtually impossible to predict with certainty the outcome of ongoing projects and their final effect on this area.

A prosperous country such as Britain should be able to find solutions to all its problems. This area has no choice but to change. Coal is no longer king and other heavy industries have declined with it. The area has so far missed the opportunity to attract major employers such as the automotive manufacturer and their potential for thousands of jobs.

Apparently the best hope we have is for a number of smaller industries to be attracted to the area. It is likely that there will be a variety of businesses, and where possible, "green" sustainable development which will require innovative skills and encompass the new technologies.

We were fortunate in 1992 when Jonathon Smales came with a vision of a possible future; an ambitious multi-million pounds project, the Earth Centre, to be developed on the former Cadeby Colliery site. It has had a stop-go existence, but now that work is again in progress, it is hoped that it will play a major role in the renaissance of the Dearne Valley as well as Conisbrough and Denaby. In the long term it could help to attract sustainable enterprises and release the energy and talent of local people in an attractive and socially acceptable environment. The residents of this community must take every opportunity to benefit from the project's potential.

Finally we must remember that the difficulties which faced our ancestors were also as great in the context of their time. They ensured that Conisbrough and Denaby survived over 14 centuries of mixed fortunes. It is now our turn to ensure the continual improvement to our future.

Bibliography

SALWAY, Peter. Roman Britain, Oxford, 1981

STENTON, Sir Frank. Anglo-Saxon England, Oxford, 1971

POOLE, Austin. From Domesday Book to Magna Carta, Oxford, 1955

WILLIAMSON, David. Kings and Queens of England, Webb and Bower, 1991

FARMER, D.H. Bede - Ecclesiastial History of the English People, Penguin

The Yorkshire Domesday, Printed Alects, Historical Editions, 1992

BERNSTEEN, David. The Mysery of the Bayeux Tapestry, Guild Publishing, 1986

MACFARLANE, J.E. The Bag Muck Strike, Denaby Main 1902-03, 1987

SMITH, Henry E. The History of Conisbrough Castle, Smith, 1887

MACFARLANE, J.E. Coalminers, Glassworkers and Potters, Doncaster Library Srevice, 1984

COWEN, Brain. and Canon C. F. Braithwaite, Conisbrough: Church and Castle, Monks, 1975

JOHNSON, Stephen M.A. Conisbrough Castle, H.M.S.O., 1984

Some Notes on Old Conisbrough, Doncater Library Service, 1985

GWATKIN, John A. A Photographic Record of the Old Village of Denaby Main, Gwatkin, 1990

SMITH, A.H. (ed.) The Place Names of the West Riding of Yorkshire, Cambridge V.P., 1952

RYDER, P.F. Saxon Churches in South Yorkshire, South Yorksire Archaeological Service, 1982